HEARTLAND

COMMON SENSE;

by Martin Capages, Jr. PhD

ADDRESSED TO THE
INHABITANTS
of
AMERICA,
on the following interesting
SUBJECTS.

I. CREATION AND EVOLUTION
II. CLIMATE CHANGE HOOEY
III. COVID
1V. CHINA

"Freedom is never more than one generation away from extinction. We did not pass it to our children in the bloodstream. It must be fought for, protected, and handed on for them to do the same." — RONALD REAGAN

SPRINGFIELD MISSOURI
AMERICAN FREEDOM PUBLICATIONS, LLC

MMXXI

© 2021 MARTIN CAPAGES JR.

All rights reserved. No part of this book may be reproduced or utilized in any form or by any means, electronic or mechanical, including photocopying, recording or by any information storage retrieval system without permission in writing from the publisher, except for a reviewer who may quote brief passages in a review to be printed in a newspaper, magazine or electronic publication.

American Freedom Publications LLC

www.americanfreedompublications.com

2638 E. Wildwood Road

Springfield 65804

ISBN 978-0-578-96597-0 Paperback Version

ISBN 978-0-578-96598-7 eBook Version

Cover Design: Christopher. M. Capages

www.capagescreative.com

First Edition-August 28, 2021

Printed in the United States of America

TABLE OF CONTENTS

PREFACE 2
I. CREATION AND EVOLUTION 3
II. CLIMATE CHANGE HOOEY 4
III. COVID 13
IV. CHINA 18
COMMON SENSE CULTURE 20
WHO OR WHAT ARE WE FIGHTING AGAINST? 28
WHAT CAN WE DO? 36
    THE EDUCATION BATTLEGROUND 38
        CRITICAL RACE THEORY 38
        REFOCUS ON FACE-TO-FACE EDUCATION 40
        GET INVOLVED 42
    STAND UP FOR AMERICAN VALUES 42
        THE DECLARATION OF INDEPENDENCE (AGAIN) ... 43
ABOUT THE AUTHOR 46
REFERENCES AND WORKS CITED 47

PREFACE

We are never going to agree about everything. It is our nature not to. To advance in understanding, one must be a skeptic. To think critically involves questioning. You must be skeptical of what you are being told in order to prevent being innocently *or purposely* misled. And that usually takes courage since there is little upside to being a skeptic. Skeptics appear to be uncommon creatures in this now Orwellian world being advanced by Progressives. First of all, if you are indeed a skeptic, you will seem to be outnumbered. By definition, you will not be a member of the consensus--the so-called majority. Second, you will be scorned, ridiculed and reviled. Third, you will be ostracized and suffer excommunication from the press and social media. And finally, you may become lonely or angry, perhaps both.

But take heart. Your Heartland Common Sense that seems to go counter to the consensus view of things means that you are an explorer and a developing leader. There is no top slot in a consensus. They all agree with each other, even if they are wrong. You see, skepticism is a meritocracy. There is no modern "equity" in it. So, of course, there is no boredom in skepticism. It is an adventure. Skeptics are seekers of the Truth. And at the end of it all, that is what matters.

Martin Capages Jr. PhD

Author of *THE MORAL CASE FOR AMERICAN FREEDOM*

I. CREATION AND EVOLUTION

"I don't know if we have a destiny, or if we're all just floatin' around accidental-like on a breeze, but I, I think maybe it's both. Maybe both is happenin' at the same time." Forrest Gump

If you want to get into a never-ending debate, this is the one. There can be no middle ground, so there will never be a consensus. There are two questions that set the field. Did we just happen and develop further through serendipity over a very, very long period of time? Or were we designed by an intelligent being or an omnipotent spirit, God? Those are the intrenched positions on the matter.

My position on the matter, after much research, academics, study, religious reading and prayer is YES.

"That's about all I got to say bout that." Forrest Gump

II. CLIMATE CHANGE HOOEY

Nullius addictus iurare in verba magistri
(Be skeptical of the experts) ---Horace

Let's start at the basics, the American desire for independence represented by the automobile. There is nothing more representative of the American spirit than the freedom derived from driving a car to any destination you want at any time that you want. Thanks to many entrepreneurs such as Henry Ford and John D. Rockefeller, the internal combustion engine or ICE, using gasoline or diesel became the predominate power source for most modes of transportation. So, the combination of fossil fuels and the internal combustion engine became the beating heart of transportation, *and still is*.

Coal-fired steam engines and gas-fired steam turbines are not ICEs. They use external combustion to turn the utility companies' generators. Gas turbines are ICEs that have now prevailed in air transport, primarily due to their higher power to weight ratios. And the fast response capability of a natural gas-fired turbine power plant is becoming a necessity to offset the intermittent nature of unreliable renewable energy sources, *e.g.*, solar and wind farms. But the conventional internal combustion gasoline engine remains as the primary power plant for America and the world's automobiles and trucks.

The world-wide manufacturing and transportation infrastructure including roadways, fueling stops, and parts suppliers is dedicated to the internal combustion engine. But there is a new entry. Actually, it is a modernized older competitor, the electric-powered automobile. The electric motor is less mechanically complex than a gasoline engine. That is actually an understatement. The internal combustion engine or ICE is an order of magnitude higher in its complexity. It has taken a century for the internal combustion engine to reach its current state of reliability, affordability and availability. Micro-electronic controls have made the ICE more fuel efficient, but the trade-off has been the elimination of the "shade tree mechanic." It is now "plug and play." The micro-computer is running the show now. If a part quits working, just replace it. Providing that specific part has become a major American industry, all built around the internal combustion engine.

So, the reintroduction of the electric car in the form of Elon Musk's Tesla and the even more radical self-driving autos and delivery trucks presents a true paradigm shift in transportation and logistics. But what about catastrophic climate change? Isn't that why we needed to change to all electric cars and trucks in the first place?

Climate alarmists have concluded that the world must reduce its generation of carbon dioxide gas or CO_2 in order to slow the current rate of increase in the average global atmospheric temperature. To do this, they are recommending the elimination of all fossil fuels as an energy source. This is a silly idea and is based on a false hypothesis. But according to Barack Obama, 97 percent of all scientists agree with this stupid hypothesis. He is wrong. More about that later.

Reducing fossil fuel use by immediately switching to electric cars is a misguided notion. The electric car requires batteries or some form of energy storage. And batteries have to be charged. Current battery design is based on lead, lithium and liquid electrolytes. They have a finite life. They are heavy and they are very expensive. They require lengthy amounts of time to recharge. Environmentally safe disposal of spent batteries is already becoming a problem. There are other electrical storage technologies which may become available such as super capacitors. These would be lighter in weight, use less exotic materials, have faster recharging rates and last much longer. But that technology is not available yet. So today, it is batteries, mostly the lithium-ion type.

Electric cars have three major problems, batteries, limited charging stations and the primary source of electrical power-*the power plant.* There is a fourth problem, affordability. That is due to the cost of cobalt and rare earth metals, notably neodymium used for electric motors. But for now, we will focus on the biggest problem, the source of the electricity to power the electric car--the power plant. *Where does the energy come from?*

Today, over eighty percent of utility service electricity in the United States is from fossil fuel-fired power plants. Hydroelectric and nuclear plants provide the bulk of the remainder with a small contribution from geothermal and biofuels. Solar and wind farms are being added to the list but are intermittent and dilute sources that require back-up from the other sources. Their meager 4% penetration into the market has increased overall power costs and added to emissions. Though called renewables, they are hardly that. There is no truly renewable energy source *and never will be.* That would be akin to having a perpetual motion machine. The problem is the physics, basically, the laws of thermodynamics. There will always be trade-offs. To go all out for electrification means that something has to provide power to recharge those batteries in the projected massive numbers of new electric cars and trucks.

There is something inherently romantic about the electric car. And it will probably prevail over the ICE auto for land transport, both personal and freight eventually. There will most likely be a hybrid phase which creates a bit more complexity but certainly is fuel efficient. But that technology, the hybrid, is here today. The transition from gasoline powered vehicles to electric-only should be based on economics, not political interference in the marketplace. And this is where "following the money" becomes important.

It is my personal opinion that the United Nations is corrupt and has contributed to more problems in the world than it has resolved. So, if you truly follow the money, you have to look into the United Nations "oil for food" scam that began with the late Maurice Strong. Then you have to analyze the mind of Al Gore, assuming you can find it, his mind that is. Following that you have to dissect the anti-Constitutional behaviors of Congressman Markey and Senator Whitehouse that culminated in the asinine Green New Deal of Democratic Socialist Alexandria Ocasio-Cortez. All of this aided by Barack Obama's claims that climate change was an existential threat to the world and that carbon dioxide was a pollutant. *What nonsense.* But in politics money flows in many deep and dark rivers, rarely achieving anything worthwhile.

And so, the river of dark money flows from both the "religious" environmentalists and the "renewables" industry to the morally weakest politicians. There has even been a fossil-fuel traitor of sorts in the domestic fossil-fuel energy crowd, the natural gas industry itself. This consortium employed a strategy that uses the "reducing CO2" mantra to hammer its major hydrocarbon competitor, the US coal industry. That has proven to be a gigantic mistake. It just shifted the target from coal to natural gas pipelines and fracking. Coal is still being mined but a lot of it is going to China. The natural gas industry's sneaky advantage over coal will be short-lived. Sneaky is as sneaky does. Politicians are even more sneaky than the natural gas industry. It is hard to produce natural gas without drilling on public lands and conducting hydraulic fracturing of shale formations. So, when you support a politician who says he is going to ban both drilling and fracking, you get what you paid for. But what do I know?

The flow of cash, though very dark, is also invisible to the main stream media. They ignore massive subsidies flooding the renewable industry and clamor about the trickle of ancient tax breaks enjoyed by industries that have assets subject to depletion like the timber and fossil fuel industry. The depletion allowance was supposed to help those industries whose livelihood was based on a finite supply of materials to sell. It is a tax deduction, not a subsidy. If someone would just report the truth about the difference between subsidies and tax breaks, that would be informative to the public. But that is a pipe dream. There is no honest investigative journalism to be found. It was forced out by the swelling of egos seeking to re-live old Washington Post Pulitzer glories. It would be great to see that old investigative zeal arise from the ashes, refocus on the facts and reject the fawning far-left media types on cable and broadcast television. But it isn't just journalists who have been compromised by the flow of money and the limelight. So have the scientists.

It is difficult to fathom the convoluted thought processes in a scientist's mind that would lead him to the conclusion that a naturally occurring gas, a necessary component of life, is somehow a pollutant. But that's what John Holdren, Obama's chief scientist managed to do without a bit of push back from the media or the scientific community. I guess the scientists Hoped there would be Change. They *hoped* that other scientists would abandon the Scientific Method while they, the climate alarmists, may have *changed* the *data* to match the hypothesis.

Obama would change things all right. He made the NASA mission one of Muslim outreach. It was something about recognizing the scientific contributions of the Persians. *Yawn.* He would also elevate computer modelers to the top leadership positions at NASA, replacing faithful practitioners of the Scientific Method. Computer programming is not science. A computer is a machine. It doesn't think. It just does what it is told to do, period. And the machines were told to produce a lot of garbage under the guise of modeling the climate. The general public has no idea that they have been lied to about the accuracy of computer-generated projections of future global temperatures. These projections are off by a factor of three. And it doesn't matter what they show anyway because atmospheric CO2 has a very little effect on the temperature, but it has a great positive effect on plant growth, *a good thing.* An increase in CO2 in the atmosphere is believed to have a positive feedback effect on water vapor and water vapor is the predominate greenhouse gas. It is predominate by an order of magnitude over CO2. But water vapor creates clouds which then affects both heating and cooling. Modeling water vapor and clouds is a difficult process and hasn't been achieved to any reasonable degree of accuracy to date. Eventually, we will overcome that limitation in the models. But the fact that we haven't as yet means that we shouldn't be making major policy decisions *affecting the lives of billions of people* based on the current state-of-the-art model projections of future global temperatures.

But wasn't there a 97 percent consensus of all climate scientists that the global average temperature was increasing, and the effect would be catastrophic for the planet? Well, there really wasn't a consensus of scientists that agreed to the latter part of that statement, the catastrophe part. Several scientists agreed that the average temperature was increasing. It has increased a little over one degree C since the Little Ice Age. The majority of the scientists agreed on that because that is what the record of temperatures, *the data,* showed. The data also showed that as the average temperature increased, the oceans released more carbon dioxide gas into the atmosphere. As the CO2 was released to the atmosphere, the ocean waters became more basic (more caustic). Now that was actually based on those scientists' understanding of mathematics and the sciences of phase behavior, chemistry and the laws of thermodynamics. And it is true that for about a century, the civilized world has been increasingly adding to the amount of carbon dioxide in the atmosphere by burning fossil fuels and also burning limestone to make cement. The slight increase in carbon dioxide or CO2 from 280 parts per million (ppm) to over 400 ppm has had a positive effect on the planet. The level of CO2 could double and would likely be even more beneficial. That's what honest objective scientists, the masters-of-mathematics and physics, say about the matter. Not computer modelers of the alarmist bent.

What about Artificial Intelligence or AI you say? Pay attention to the first word, Artificial. The more computer power you have, the more intelligent it seems, but it is still artificial. However, the computer is still faster than you are in analyzing data, lots and lots of data. But it has to be told how to analyze the data in the first place. That's the job of the computer programmer and/or modeler. There is a difference between a programmer and a modeler, but we won't dwell on it here. Just understand that computer programmers are on the "geeky" side while the computer modelers are more uppity and think they are special branch of science. In truth, they are a lesser branch but appear to be more glamorous to the media than physicists, geologists, and ecologists.

Under the Obama administration, the far-left anti-fossil fuel environmental and renewables industry lobbies went to work on the weakest of the Democrats. They needed the specter of Al Gore's catastrophic global warming to stay in power. That set the funding of government and university research to be directed to programs advancing the catastrophe narrative even though that narrative was discredited by the actual data. Corruptive influences in the computer modeling community even led to altering the data to comply with the hypothesis. Some of the modelers took over the scientific community leadership and controlled all research publications. It was shameful but profitable. Now if you wanted a government grant, you better believe (or pretend) that there is climate catastrophe out there or you won't receive any funding from the government. If you want more information on that corruption, read Andy May's book POLITICS AND CLIMATE CHANGE: A History. (May, 2020)

That is only a glimpse of the money trail. There is another major influencer promoting the anti-fossil fuel movement-*China*. And that is going to be a longer and convoluted story.

In the United States, onerous regulations, cutting oil and gas exploration and production leases on federal lands, closing ANWR, stopping pipelines, frivolous lawsuits, and banks constricting the flow of capital under the banner of ESG (Environmental, social, and governance criteria) *is going to increase energy costs.* ESG is an anti-capitalism, anti-free market movement of mis-guided elitists who are in control of the World's purse strings. ESG pushes a set of standards for a company's operations that "socially conscious investors" are supposed to use to screen potential investments. It is top down virtual signaling for an un-elected high-level leadership. ESG is the China Trap.

In theory, the ESG criteria is used to rate how a company performs as a steward of nature, shareholders interested in the rate of return on capital employed are ignored. Cowardly CEOs and takeovers of corporate boards by environmental activists have caused the constriction of the supply of investment capital and raised its costs, in particular the capital needed by America's fossil fuel industry. But not everywhere. Not in China for sure. The top three highest revenue oil companies in the world are now controlled by the communist Chinese. This year, 2021 or next, China will become the world's largest oil refiner. They are building refineries. We haven't built a new refinery in decades. While the United States and the West are constricting their oil industry, communist China is growing theirs. Russia is following the lead of the CCP and will soon have Europe captive to Russian gas. The Germans need natural gas desperately because of their over-commitment to wind and solar farms and the havoc this unreliable, intermittent duo creates in management of their electrical grid. Energy poverty in Germany is a real thing. (Epstein, 2019)

But China? Oh my. China is quietly taking the lead in oil, natural gas, and coal because the CCP leadership understands that the nearly 40 billion barrels of oil used each year provides reliable, affordable, and abundant energy. Their awakening economy must have more energy or there will be a revolution. Energy fuels the machines that fuel the economy. Beijing knows that much, if not all, of the World's wind and solar system components will likely be supplied by . . .China. At the same time China's emissions of all pollutants will soon surpass all of the developed nations combined. The Chinese goal for 2049 is to be the Masters of the Universe, or at least the part of the Universe earth occupies now. As they launch missions to Mars, our own NASA is focusing on Equity. Unfortunately, there will not be an equal outcome.

The Climate Change Alarmists community has become the catalyst for the destruction of America and the Western world. They have sowed the whirlwind with scientific hooey. The ignorance or perhaps the evil intent of some politicians will accelerate the fall of America into the rule of an elitist class of AOC's Social Democrats---the pigs of Animal Farm, all in the name of Climate Change. (Capages Jr., 2020)

III. COVID

Epidemiology is a medical and biological science. According to Wikipedia "Epidemiology is the study and analysis of the distribution (who, when, and where), patterns and determinants of health and disease conditions in defined populations."

However, the purposeful creation of an epidemic is a tactic of warfare, *ancient warfare*. While biological warfare has been banned by the United Nations, no nation can dismiss it outright as a matter of defense. Preventing a global pandemic, though altruistic, has the same goal as a biological warfare defense. But that requires prediction of the characteristics of the biological agent you want to defend against. Some believe that to defend against a biological agent, you must first create one.

The December 2019 corona virus was developed in a Chinese military research laboratory in Wuhan, China that was conducting "gain of function" research on a coronavirus specific to a species of bats. "Gain of function" means changing the biological characteristics of a biological pathogen to increase its ability to spread into humans. In the fall of 2019, the necessary safety protocols were broken, researchers were contaminated, and the virus was spread throughout the world. The result was the COVID 19 Pandemic that has killed over 600 thousand Americans with over 2 million casualties worldwide and is still spreading.

"Gain of function" research may be continuing in the US, China and Russia. It is unlikely that an international ban on such research would have any effect. The research would likely continue in secret. With that in mind, the lessons from the American response to the COVID-19

Pandemic should be carefully analyzed. The Nation suffered and it didn't need to suffer as much as it did. There is blame to share, but is there courage to do so?

The American response was hindered by partisan politics at a time when all action should have been bipartisan and in support of the Chief Executive. This was a time to set aside the bickering between political parties and to get to work to solve the problem. But that didn't happen. What happened was political theater of the worst kind perpetrated by the Democratic Party leadership and the anti-Trump mainstream media. When the responsible thing to do was to focus on the coming pandemic, the Pelosi-controlled Congress focused on the impeachment of a President *already out of office*. The actual shenanigans were detailed in my book *PERSISTENT EVIL—SOCIALISM: A Warning for the Millennial Generation* so there is no need to repeat that dark bit of recent history. What needs to be understood is that this pandemic provided useful information for Chinese military war planning, not just epidemiological research. Many democracies suffered disastrous economic losses, not just a reduction in their older population.

Here you had an airborne pathogen that was easily transmitted from human to human, not just by physical contact. The pathogen would use the body's immune response to attack itself in a rapid fashion. It was initially a pulmonary attack, not a slow-moving blood disorder.

It is clear that the pathogen was manufactured in a Chinese biological research facility in Wuhan, China. This research facility was and still is a part of the Chinese military machine. *All Chinese research is*. It is unlikely that the *early* release of the pathogen was planned and was probably accidental. But the steps that followed were evil. The CCP knew the virus spread by *human-to-human* contact. The Chinese authorities remedy to lock-down the local population, curtail travel inside China while still allowing international travel out of Wuhan created many problems for the international community. The fact that the United Nations World Health Organization was involved in the both the development of the corona virus mutant strain and the cover-up is one of those many problems. The partial funding of the "gain of function" by American taxpayers is also a big, big problem. But it gets worse.

The Chinese took action to acquire the available World supply of personal protective equipment, PPE, for exclusive use in China before announcing the contagious nature of the virus and its lethality. But poor messaging by the United States authorities and medical experts magnified the severity of the contagion in the eyes of the general public. The US mainstream media pushed Chinese propaganda on the source of the virus and downplayed the effectiveness of early treatment and preventative measures such as the anti-Malarial drug Hydroxychloroquine. The Chinese would control the supply of this drug while Big Pharma sought more expensive options for early treatment and preventative measures including vaccines. There was a guaranteed profit since the U. S. Government was eliminating all risk to Big Pharma. The epicenter for the early outbreak in the US would be New York City where incompetent state and local leadership and political partisanship would cause many deaths in the older population that could have been prevented.

With the panic came the government lock-downs on the economy and a major disruption of the supply chain. Hoarding of toilet paper, medical masks and hand sanitizers was the result. It has now become the American Way today. That didn't use to be the way Americans behaved.

MASK ON-MASK OFF

-Apologies to Mr. Miyagi-

Added to the controversy of self-quarantining and social distancing was the question of wearing face masks. The first government guidance was that masks were unnecessary. Then it was masks should be worn. It was explained that the earlier guidance was to prevent a run-on masks and other PPE that would be needed by medical personnel treating the victims of COVID. First it was N95 masks, then surgical masks, then cloth masks, even homemade ones. Then it was all school kids must wear masks, all the time in school and outside, even in outdoor athletic competition. None of this was very smart. Surgical and cloth masks do not prevent or even slow down the spread of the virus. Properly worn N95 respirators may to some extent but they do not protect the eyes. That takes goggles or face shields. It is unlikely that the general public would be able to have the discipline to wear N95 masks and all the other paraphernalia in the proper manner or even have access to this PPE. And forcing grade schoolers to wear cloth masks that will do them no good and may cause significant harm both mentally and physically is a cause for concern to parents. An excellent analysis of the facts on mask use was written by Alex Berenson in November 2020. (Berenson, 2020) More information is now available, but it is not being used in policy making. The Heartland problem with masking is not whether they are effective or not. It is a matter of Individual Freedom versus an authoritarian State Mandate.

We used to be courageous and brave, willing to help others in time of need. Now many Americans have become "preppers", hiding in their basements with AR-15s and stock piles of ammunition and canned food. *Ridiculous.* We can and must be smarter than that. When we have to defend ourselves from ourselves, the battle is over. We must identify the enemy in order to defend against it. The Chinese now have the information to see how defenseless the West is against a biological warfare pathogen. They are communists. They do not see humanity as individuals, they believe the survival of the collective is more important than individual lives. The use of biological warfare in a global conflict is not going to be restricted by an agreement between nations. It never will be. The CCP will always seek the advantage even if it is deemed evil by Western culture. To them, agreements are things that can be broken.

What if the next pandemic is caused by a natural or artificial pathogen that is spread by physical contact with the skin or by oral consumption, not through the air? Now the necessary PPE would be different. There would be a run-on Tyvek Hazmat suits and duct tape. A gallon of clean water could become as valuable as gold or maybe even as valuable as a gallon of gasoline. You can't eat gold. It takes gasoline to power a portable generator at night or when the wind stops blowing. But many American politicians are working to eliminate gasoline or make it even more expensive with an artificial tax called the Carbon Tax. Some know what they are doing, others are going along for the ride. It will be a ride to oblivion for the United States of America.

IV. CHINA

China is not a future problem for the free world. It is a problem today. That is evident in their involvement in the COVID-19 Pandemic discussed in Chapter III. The CCP intends to become the World's hegemony. The Chinese people are not going to rise-up and overthrow their communist overlords. It is too late. The pure inertia of nearly 2 billion people mesmerized by Group-Think and Thought-Control cannot be forced off course with diplomacy or rhetoric. It will take a forceful resistance of outsiders using every means possible to reverse 75 years of brain-washing. But the resistance does not have to be by force of arms. It can be through digital communications. But the digital advantage of the West is fading fast.

The American political leadership is falling into the trap of domestic tunnel vision. Our intelligence services are being directed to investigate our own citizens, not external subversive elements. The Judicial system has become unbalanced and has even become a tool of the left in the suppression of political dissent by conservatives. This is playing directly into the hands of the Chinese Communist Party. We cannot defend the Nation by diluting our intelligence resources. The enemy is not within the American Heartland, it is in Asia.

China is not a Western culture. It is a massive population of innocent people who have been historically brutalized by other nations and by their own leadership. They are just re-entering the modern world and are susceptible to state-sponsored media and its propaganda. Much as Goebbels did for the Nazis, the CCP propaganda machine is reminding the people of the past and current abuses inflicted on them by the outside world. It does not give them time to reflect on the actual self-inflicted pain of Mao Tsung and his Cultural Revolution. That revolutionary insanity claimed the lives of several million people and inflicted cruel and inhuman treatments on hundreds of millions of people. However, 40 years after it ended, the total number of victims of the Cultural Revolution and especially the death toll of mass killings still remains a mystery both in China and overseas. The mystery is perpetuated by the CCP but it is clear that over 3 million Chinese died while millions of Chinese suffered enormously and gained nothing. But the collective survives. The Chinese Communist Party continues to carry out human rights abuses against Uighurs, ethnic Kazakhs and members of other minority groups in Xinjiang. The abuses include forced labor, arbitrary mass detention, forced population control, and attempts to erase their culture. That qualifies the Chinese to be on the Human Rights Committee of the UN, right? They *know* how to handle human rights.

The real power of the Chinese has been in the area of finance and exploiting the moral weakness of their takeover targets. Throughout Asia, the Chinese bankers have moved into strategic positions, using tactics that include bribery and financial acuity. Dark money flows into the political campaign war chests of those they believe they can control now or will eventually be able to control by way of blackmail. In the election of 2020, they were able to take down an opposing US president with a two-pronged attack of a Chinese corona virus, COVID-19 and financial support of voter manipulation efforts, both the old monetary payoff kind and perhaps the manipulation of voting machines. They were aided by Big Tech which has no loyalty to Americans and our value system. Corporate greed has supplanted patriotism in most of America, but not the Heartland. But the physical owners of the rural Heartland, our farms, will soon be Chinese unless we wake up to the danger.

COMMON SENSE CULTURE

It is becoming clearer each day that the American electorate made a big mistake in the Presidential Election of 2020. Nearly half the country believes the election was illicit, but that belief is not going to change the circumstances. The far-left Progressives have gained control of the government and their goal is to make America a utopian socialistic society. Equity or equality of outcome has replaced Equal Opportunity, one of the foundations of the American Dream. Equity does not mean Equal Justice under the Law. It means the Justice will be manipulated to produce the result desired by those in Power.

The story of Progressivism is long and sordid. Progressivism today is not the modernization of government as many believe. Progressivism is a process to convert the government of the United States from a representative republic with a free market economy to an oligarchical technology-driven dictatorship with a socialistic economy. The government will control the means of production and the distribution of products to the masses. Unfortunately, elites in power will always skim off the cream at the top and the masses will receive the dregs. That is the history of Marxism and always has been.

While those currently in power in the American government believe that they know best, they are not wise. It takes humility to be wise, to learn from one's mistakes, and to make corrections. But humility is counter to the political mindset. A cloak of Patriotism can help one to gain political office and access to power but is often discarded by those with low morality. The exploitation of race and class envy are tools to gain advantage. These are set aside while in office but are pulled from the political toolkit when an election is on the horizon. Unfortunately, these are the primary tools of the Democratic Party. It is clear that patriotism and wisdom are lacking in the likes of the Squad, Maxine Waters, Mazie Hirono and Nancy Pelosi. It is not racial bigotry or misogynistic to point out stupidity, ignorance or perhaps, stubbornness. If it isn't those three possibilities, then all that is left is an evil, unsatiable quest for power, prestige, and financial reward.

Joe Biden is living up to predictions that he would be unable to resist the opportunity provided by a narrow political margin to move America to the far left. He said he would be the most Progressive president in history as though that was something glorious. It isn't. This meant a spiteful undoing of all his predecessor's positive policies that were benefiting the economy and the people in general. Joe Biden is unqualified for the job, is in cognitive decline, but is protected by his staff and the media. They know far too well his penchant for gaffs and angry outbursts when facing a substantive question. He is a shell of a President, but his under-study, Kamala Harris, is even less qualified for the job and has a history of poor performance. All of his cabinet officers and department heads are misfit activists aligned with or owned by Beijing, or perhaps both. The Biden Administration, the Democratic Party and the mainstream media have become detached from reality. The country is in extreme danger now and will be for the next three years.

But the Common Sense of the American Heartland is a real thing. We can head off this slide into Socialism. We begin with the belief that the United States of America is still a righteous nation. This is important since the alternative is Rule by the State. You either believe in the Founding Principles of this nation or you do not. If you do not believe in these Principles, then it is likely that you haven't been taught the true early history of the United States of America. If that is not the case and you are aware of the Nation's early history but do not respect the Founding Principles, *then perhaps you shouldn't be in this country*. But it would be better for you if you would reconsider the Founding Principles and change your mind. Giving up individual freedom based on petulance is a poor trade.

In my first book, *The Moral Case for American Freedom*, I provided a considerable amount of evidence that the true Spirit of America was built upon Judeo-Christian principles. But we are in deep trouble now. Perhaps we can restore the Nation by returning to those principles. It does not matter if you are a believer, agnostic or atheist. The Founders of the Nation trusted in the Bible for spiritual and practical guidance. Both Christians and those of the Jewish faith are guided by the Old Testament. It doesn't matter if it is the Old Testament or the New Testament. The followers of Christ recognize that the Christ of the New Testament was a Hebrew and honored the Old Testament scriptures. The majority of the American Heartland believes that the United States of America was chosen by God to do His Will. It is the Heartland's great Hope.

PSALM 33: 12-22 (NIV)

Blessed is the nation whose God is the Lord, the people He chose for His inheritance.
From heaven the Lord looks down and sees all mankind; from His dwelling place He watches all who live on earth—
He Who forms the hearts of all, Who considers everything they do.
No king is saved by the size of his army; no warrior escapes by his great strength.

A horse is a vain hope for deliverance; despite all its great strength it cannot save.

But the eyes of the Lord are on those who fear Him, on those whose hope is in His unfailing love, to deliver them from death and keep them alive in famine.

We wait in hope for the Lord; He is our help and our shield. In Him our hearts rejoice, for we trust in His Holy Name.

May Your Unfailing Love be with us, Lord, even as we put our hope in You.

But much like the Prodigal Son, the Nation has resisted the guidance of the Bible and is becoming more and more secular. While secularism is defined as an indifference to or rejection or exclusion of religion and religious considerations, it has morphed into a principle of separation of religion from civic affairs and the state or even the removal or minimalization of the role of religion in government or any public area. "Separation of church and state" is paraphrased from Thomas Jefferson and used by others in expressing an understanding of the intent and function of the Establishment Clause and Free Exercise Clause of the First Amendment to the United States Constitution which reads: "Congress shall make no law respecting an establishment of religion, or prohibiting the free exercise thereof..." This is the subject of much debate even today. The idea was to prevent the establishment of a State sponsored religion. But the Supreme Court found that the Nation's "institutions presuppose a Supreme Being" and that government recognition of God does not constitute the establishment of a state church as the Founders intended to prohibit.

While all of this is important, it is also important to recognize that the American Heartland has been guided in the past by its Judeo-

Christian belief system which is inculcated in the Law of the Land. The first step then to restoring the Nation is clear.

2 CHRONICLES 7:14 (NIV)

If My people, who are called by My Name, will humble themselves and pray and seek My face and turn from their wicked ways, then I will hear from heaven, and I will forgive their sin and will heal their land.

The early American settlers were predominately Christians, mostly Protestants seeking a new life, to escape both religious and other types of persecution. Many of the settlers were aristocrats with wealthy sponsors. Others were indentured servants, and some were African slaves that were brought into the land by the Dutch and British. The settlers were successful economically and declared their independence from Britain in 1776. They won that independence in 1783. In the summer of 1787, the colonies, now States, wrote a constitution that was like none other ever conceived. The preamble to the U. S. Constitution says:

We the People of the United States, in Order to form a more perfect Union, establish Justice, ensure domestic Tranquility, provide for the common defense, promote the general Welfare, and secure the Blessings of Liberty to ourselves and our Posterity, do ordain and establish this Constitution for the United States of America.

The Preamble was placed in the Constitution during the last days of the Constitutional Convention by the Committee on Style, which wrote its final draft, with Gouverneur Morris leading the effort. (Mironuck, 2017)

The final draft of the completed Constitution was presented to the convention on September 12, 1787, contained seven articles, the preamble and a closing endorsement, of which Morris was the primary author. This whole effort was overseen by George Washington himself.

On June 21, 1788, the Constitution was ratified by the minimum of nine states required under Article VII. Towards the end of July, and with eleven states then having ratified, the process of organizing the new government began. The Continental Congress, which still functioned at irregular intervals, passed a resolution on September 13, 1788, to put the new Constitution into operation with the eleven states that had then ratified it. The federal government began operations under the new form of government on March 4, 1789. George Washington was inaugurated as the nation's first president on April 30, 1789. *The new Constitution did not resolve the issue of slavery.* To get a final agreement, a compromise between the interests of the Southern and Northern States was necessary. The Constitution was a framework for mutual governance for five free states and eight slave states. The way the framers secured this difficult union was to create a federal government of limited powers that had no jurisdiction to govern the domestic affairs of the individual states.

The travesty of slavery would lead to a civil war between the Northern and Southern states. The North would prevail in 1865, all slaves were freed, and slavery would be banned forever more in the United States of America. The transition from slavery to freedom was just that, a transition. It didn't happen instantly at the end of the Civil War. It would take a hundred years to enshrine Civil Rights into the Nation's conscience. That is the history until now.

Today we have a new phenomenon. American society has undergone a fundamental cultural shift that has desensitized people to the destruction of human life. This has occurred in the more secular areas of the Nation, the main population centers. The culture now devalues and degrades human life through entertainment, drugs, pornography, abortion, and the rejection of morality. There is rampant disrespect for the dignity of other people and for human life in general. According to the former Governor of Kentucky, Matt Bevin: "We're desensitizing people to the value of life. And we see it through the lyrics in music. And we see it through television shows and we see it through movies. We see it in the fact that the morays of this nation have changed. And we see it through the fact that we increasingly want to remove any sense of moral authority from everything." The Governor is right.

The common Sense of the American Heartland is founded on its inherent culture values. "There are three pairs of values consisting of three reasons why immigrants have come (and still do) to the United States and three prices that are paid for these benefits. The values and prices paid to achieve these values are:

Individual Freedom and Self-Reliance

Equality of Opportunity and Competition

The American Dream and Hard Work

The first value is Individual Freedom and the price for that is Self-Reliance. We cannot be truly free if we cannot take care of ourselves and be independent. The second value is Equality of Opportunity, and the price for that is Competition. If everyone has an equal chance for success, then we have to compete. The third value is The American Dream, the opportunity for a better life and a higher standard of living. The price for the American Dream has traditionally been Hard Work."

These six basic cultural values are contrary to the concepts of "diversity, equity and inclusion" that have been embraced by the far-left Democratic Socialist wing of Democratic Party. It is a matter of the Power of the State versus Individual Freedom. The Common Sense of the American Heartland is based on Individual Freedom. At its founding, Americans fought to be free and rallied under the banner "Live Free or Die." We will do so again.

WHO OR WHAT ARE WE FIGHTING AGAINST?

You cannot win a battle or achieve the ultimate victory without first identifying the enemy. The obvious external enemy is the Chinese Communist Party, the CCP. The internal enemy was well described by Lee Smith in an interview with Tucker Carlson on his Tucker Carlson Today show (available on FoxNation). Smith says, "The United States has an Occupation Government." He is referring to the Establishment Elite. Their goal is the Global Community, a utopia where there are no nations, no cultural impediments, and no religions of any kind. But it is clear there can be no Global Community that does not include China. However, China is not the Chinese people. China is the CCP and the CCP does not want a Global Community. The CCP wants a Global Chinese Communist Party totalitarian state. And they plan to have it by 2049.

The Occupation Government of the United States that Lee Smith was referring to is very real. It was put in place by the Elite Establishment, mostly with good intentions but naïve to human nature. To achieve the Global goal, over the last few decades the Establishment has aligned with institutions that have been overwhelmingly corrupted by closet Marxists in the media and academia and, more recently, by the CCP.

Major private and public corporations have been compromised. Even Congress has Democratic Socialists that are now openly professing Socialism as their preferred form of governing. They are "useful idiots" being played by the Chinese. Useful idiots are groups of people who use propaganda to drive a cause without fully comprehending the cause's goals. Useful idiots are cynically used by the goal setter. Congressperson

Alexandria Ocasio-Cortez and her Green New Deal supporters fit that definition. She is either ignorant or corrupt. Ignorance can be overcome with education and experience, but there has to be a desire to seek the Truth. Corruption cannot be overcome that way. Corruption is a tool used by the Chinese. They are masters at the game. And we have to call out the Biden Family as one of those corrupted institutions, they are the "most useful idiots" of the CCP.

Joe Biden has no business being the President of the United States. He is unqualified mentally and morally. According to Barack Obama, "Don't underestimate Joe's ability to F#%& it up." The media certainly overestimated Biden's mental acuity or intentionally covered it up. Obama's Secretary of Defense, Robert Gates was fairly blunt when discussing Biden's understanding of world affairs. In chronicling his time as the Secretary of Defense, Gates said Biden had been "wrong on nearly every major foreign policy and national security issue over the past four decades." Biden's string of foreign policy blunders continues.

But his moral compass or lack thereof is evident in domestic affairs as well. He may even have been a segregationist in his early political career. He certainly supported segregationists in the Democratic Party. He professes to be a practicing Catholic but supports late term and post-birth abortion. He is the head of the Biden family in the same vein as Don Vito Corleone but without the smarts. However, the Biden family and the Biden administration are protected by many other corrupt organizations such as academia, major corporations, the mainstream press, Hollywood elites, social media giants-Big Tech, and the DNC. This is so obvious that it has become boring to most of America. Especially since American patriots can't seem to do anything about it even in the National electoral process. That too has been corrupted by the same Occupation Government described by Lee Smith. It appears that America has gone past the tipping point that the Founders were worried about from the very beginning, a government aware of itself. The government must now attack its founding documents and their enshrined "checks and balances." But the Chinese government has no "checks and balances" at all. It is completely totalitarian. And they want to be and have been very helpful in the destruction of America.

The Chinese people are now controlled by a social credit system that has been implemented just recently as a result of digital database technology. A similar system that does not have government force behind it is also being implemented in the US and most of the West. It is a digital surveillance system that has brought about the "Cancel Culture", a merger of Marxism and today's electronic social media. A Rule by the Few using Intimidation is emerging as more and more of the business of life is conducted on smart phones. And this will be difficult to undo.

The Internet is not the enemy of the People. It is the misuse of the Internet that is the destructive force. This is very much like the Second Amendment argument that "guns don't kill people, people do." Actually, it is the criminal misuse of firearms that is causing today's mayhem. Controlling the access to guns by criminals seems simple enough. But gun laws don't control criminals, gun law enforcement does. There are plenty of gun control laws. They just haven't been enforced and today, they are less likely to be enforced.

Why would anyone seek a career in law enforcement today? If the people do not support their own guardians, then they have accepted anarchism. But we are not at that point yet. It is coming though with the Biden administration's use of power to prosecute its political enemies. There is no "equality of justice under the law" when violent protestors such as BLM, Antifa and other hardened criminals are released into the community while conservative political protestors are hunted down and jailed without cause. We must fight against this abuse of power, but we must first understand its origin.

Long before the Chicoms, Marxism was a thing. It was based on a process of destruction of the existing order in order to implement a new order. Societies always fall into an order of the "haves and have-nots. The definition of the haves and the have-nots', is a classification of people. Hence the term "class." But class can be birthright, financial status, race, ethnicity, religion, gender, sexual preference and many more. The list of potential classes is endless. The Marxist approach is to pick the lowest class and pit it against the upper class. In the process, the middle class is destroyed from both ends. At the end of the class warfare, the lower class and upper class remain while the middle class no longer exists. While the idea was make to everyone the same, a predominate middle class, it always fails. The law of Entropy exists even in human relations and government.

The United States has had a robust middle-class economy. It has been untouchable by Marxism for many years. This successful economy was protected by an outstanding military with civilian leadership. The Chinese have studied this for a long time. The Chinese are Masters of Finance with a strong bent towards using the corruptive tendency or weaknesses of others while refraining from this tendency themselves. Their success in doing this, their self-discipline, is the foundation of the Communist Party. As one Chinese doctor said in reviewing the cause of the COVID 19 Pandemic, "they have no respect for the individual or any human rights." This makes them evil by definition. They know how to use human weakness, usually greed or other temptations, to place a person in a compromised position. They have identified the openness of the American system as a weakness, and they have fully exploited that openness.

It has been over fifty years since the Nixon administration, primarily Henry Kissinger, worked hard to open the closed nation of China. It was a strategy to defang the influence of the Soviet Union. It didn't work. The old Soviets and Chinese remained steadfast as communist partners. In the early 90s, the Clinton administration faced the same problem but in reverse. He wanted to make nice with the Russians to slow down the Chinese but then gave up. Instead, he decided to follow the Globalist idea of helping China become more democratic and ignored its civil rights abuses. The Tiananmen Square protests of 1989 were before Clinton's time in office. A creature of the 60s counter-culture, he was adverse to conflict. Later on, he would find the Chinese to be a source of political contributions.

In the spring of 2000, China was trying to become a member of the World Trade Organization (WTO). The U.S. House of Representatives had just approved normalizing trade relations with China. The vote was effectively a U.S. endorsement of China's accession, and President Bill Clinton, a major proponent of China's bid, voiced his economic and strategic hopes for the U.S.-China relationship.

> "Today the House of Representatives has taken an historic step toward continued prosperity in America, reform in China, and peace in the world. . . it will open new doors of trade for America and new hope for change in China." **Bill Clinton.**

But things didn't work out for the private sector labor unions in manufacturing and factory work. They opposed the WTO accession deal, since it was clear to them that cheaper labor in China would cost jobs in the United States. And they were right: between 1999 and 2011, almost 6 million U.S. manufacturing jobs were lost. A landmark study attributed nearly 1 million of those manufacturing job losses, and 2.4 million total job losses, to competition from China. Today, it is much worse.

In 2000, then Senator Joe Biden voted in favor of normalizing trade relations with China and supported China's entry into the World Trade Organization. Both he and Bill Clinton sold out the trade unions. No harm done it appears. Who needs the trade unions when you have the NEA, AFT and the other public sector unions? At this point, Biden was recognized as a friend of China and by default, the CCP. By the way, there are no private or public unions in China. Collective bargaining is unnecessary in a collective. The bargain has been made. Individual freedom has been lost.

At this time, there are very few U. S. lobbying groups, university faculties and private think tanks that are free of Chinese financial influence. And with the revolving door between Congress, Administration staff, and the lobbyists, China is in control of the Occupation Government of the United States. Those are the details of the things the Heartland must fight against. But in reality, it is just one:

MARXISM

The purveyors of Marxism are:

Social Democrats and Progressives in Congress
Black Lives Matter
Antifa
The Chinese Communist Party

The facilitators of Marxism are:

The Mainstream Media
The NEA and AFT
Big Tech
Major Corporations
Academia
The DNC and Weak Republicans

The tools being used by the Marxists are:
Division
Propaganda
Partisan Authoritarianism

The Marxists have used the notion of Diversity to divide the Nation into tribal groups that they can mesmerize with an overwhelming stream of propaganda designed to pit one tribe against the other. The propaganda has been imbedded into everything digital to maintain the inherent bigotry between the tribes. For an individual or group to attempt to expose the lies in the propaganda will result in a politically driven prosecution by the Authoritarian state. The authorities will use criminal prosecution procedures, not civil prosecution procedures to make a public arrest then proceed with a trial before judges corrupted by political influence. Americans have witnessed this in the prosecution of Roger Stone, the investigation of Rudy Giuliani and the hunt for participants in the protests of the 2020 Presidential election that occurred at the U. S. Capitol on January 6, 2021. They have seen the FBI and the Department of Justice use procedures in violation of the laws outlined in the U. S. Constitution. The American Civil Liberties Union has remained silent. *They are misnamed.*

WHO OR WHAT ARE WE FIGHTING AGAINST?

But violent, destructive violators of the law, BLM and Antifa are not subject to the same laws it seems. They destroy private and public property with no penalties. These violators of our laws are not prosecuted. Why? Because they are a component of the Occupation Government, much like the Brown Shirts of Hitler's National Socialist German Worker's Party, the Nazis, and Mussolini's Black Shirts. The parallels are evident on video for all to see. There are protestors physically attacking the police and Federal officers with fires burning in the background. The mainstream media calls it "peaceful protests." The Democratic Party says nothing but provides funds to bail the protestors out of jail. But a legitimate protest of an election result winds up with those protestors jailed without bail. Sure, some of the protestors breached the Capitol building and that was wrong. They defeated the very objective of the protest which was to support the legislators who were in the process of conducting a legal protest according to the U. S. Constitution. One unarmed protestor was killed by the Capital Police and some officers were injured. But this was not an insurrection. It was a political protest that got hijacked by its own naivete. It is spiteful or perhaps even evil to call it an "insurrection."

The people that participated in the protests at the U. S. Capitol on January 6, 2021, were exercising their rights under the U. S. Constitution. The BLM, Antifa and anarchists who rioted and looted in the streets of America throughout 2020 and into 2021 were not legitimate protestors. Their goal was not reform. Their goal was, and still is, the destruction of America, the Republic and the values of the American Heartland. They must be stopped. And they will be.

WHAT CAN WE DO?

We can start by using our HEARTLAND COMMON SENSE. George Washington started with the written word. At a time that defeat at the hands of the great British Army appeared imminent, and the Colonists appeared to be wavering in their support of the War for Independence, English-born writer and patriot pamphleteer Thomas Paine wrote the following:

"THESE are the times that try men's souls. The summer soldier and the sunshine patriot will, in this crisis, shrink from the service of their country; but he that stands by it now, deserves the love and thanks of man and woman. Tyranny, like hell, is not easily conquered; yet we have this consolation with us, that the harder the conflict, the more glorious the triumph. What we obtain too cheap, we esteem too lightly: it is dearness only that gives every thing its value. Heaven knows how to put a proper price upon its goods; and it would be strange indeed if so celestial an article as FREEDOM should not be highly rated" — Thomas Paine, The Crisis

We won that war but would face the British once again in 1812. We would win that war as well. American Navy Commodore Oliver Hazard Perry on September 10, 1813, after defeating a British naval squadron on Lake Erie during that war would say, "We have met the enemy and they are ours." Well done, Commodore. But today it is different. Today the great swamp philosopher Pogo comes to mind. Walt Kelly's Pogo, in support of the early Earth Day activities of 1970-71 said, "We have found the Enemy and He is Us." Pogo is standing in a sea of waste and trash polluting his swamp homeland. This was of course before Earth Day was hijacked by the anti-human environmental movement.

Pogo's statement is only half-right in today's world. The enemy is half of the American voting constituency, the majority that elected Joe Biden and placed Nancy Pelosi in the position to do the most damage to the Individual Freedom of the American People. That is a very harsh critique of the first female Speaker of the House of Representatives, but it has been earned. She has placed the retention of political power before her oath to defend the Constitution of the United States of America. She has been a devious manager and a destructive force that has lacked any semblance of self-inspection or self-awareness. But she is leaving Congress in 2022 and perhaps, the self-inspection will begin as she faces her real constituency at home in San Francisco, a constituency and a House she left in shambles in her pursuit of political power.

The Heartland is all that remains of the Free Nation, The United States of America. Newsom and Pelosi's California is dying under the controlling Democratic Party rule. Why in the world do Californians keep voting for these corrupt officials? That is simple to answer. They have no access to the Truth. Where is the propaganda designed? On the East and West Coasts. Where are the broadcast and cable news stations located? Same places. Where does the Internet and Big Tech reside? Same places. Where does the Heartland cash flow go? Same places. Where does it get spent? Same places. Right, it doesn't make it to the Heartland, unless of course, there are government strings attached.

The Heartland is proud of its heritage of financial stewardship and common sense. The Red States are generally well managed. The Democrat-controlled Blue States are not. They are populated by users, not producers. So, revenue from the Red States is used to prop up the

Blue State urban centers. Rural and suburban Capitalism is supporting Urban Socialism. This can only continue when productivity increases. The arts and entertainment do not produce food and fuel. Hard Work does.

I have been and still am a supporter of the grass roots effort called the Convention of States Project. (Cherry, 2018) However, it may be too late for that noble effort to save the Nation from the scourge of Marxism. The real grass roots action has to begin in the Heartland itself at its very core, *the local school system*. America must first cross its own Delaware River to win its own Battle of Trenton to change the course of the war.

THE EDUCATION BATTLEGROUND

You have to pick your battlefield to have an advantage. The battle for the minds of most college and university students is over and the Progressives have won that initial skirmish. That was Bunker Hill. But they have also infiltrated the elementary and secondary schools. The new Minute Men are the parents of the young students. They are rallying and railing against Diversity, Equity and Inclusion personified by Cultural Marxism disguised as a movement to incorporate Critical Race Theory into the local school curriculum.

CRITICAL RACE THEORY

One of the most destructive movements that must be overcome is the introduction of Critical Race Theory (CRT) into our elementary and secondary schools. In his book *American Marxism*, author and attorney Mark Levin says, "CRT is an insidious and racist Marxist ideology spreading throughout our culture and society." In his book *Intellectuals and Society*, Dr. Thomas Sowell, author, scholar, and professor, denounces the entire multicultural/ identity politics movement. He explains that "[t]he kind of collective justice demanded for racial or ethnic groups is often espoused as 'social justice,' since it seeks to undo disparities created by circumstances, as well as those created by the injustices of human beings. Moreover, cosmic justice not only extends from individuals to groups, it extends beyond contemporary groups to intertemporal abstractions, of which today's groups are conceived as being the current embodiments."

Mark Levin wants CRT banned. Thomas Sowell explains the nature of the beast. Robert L. Woodson has a different approach which he explains as follows:

"Let me be clear about one thing up front: I think critical race theory is nonsense. Most of its proponents insist that all black people are perpetually oppressed victims, and all white people are our oppressors. This does nothing to move the black community, or our country, forward.

But unfortunately, too many conservatives are dealing with it in a way that is understandable but incomplete. Just as we wouldn't ban teaching students about communism or fascism, our schools should equip students with the intellectual tools to understand any ideology — including CRT — and decide for themselves what they think about it.

At its core, critical race theory is a perversion of the civil-rights legacy that I fought for because it minimizes the ability of each person to shape his or her own future. It bears almost no resemblance to the civil-rights message of great leaders such as Martin Luther King Jr., who envisioned a society in which everyone is treated equally before the law and held to the same standards. America is about free competition, including the free competition of ideas. CRT should neither be banned nor implemented as fact; it should, instead, be debated and scrutinized. Banning ideas only teaches our kids either to fear them or become fascinated with them. At the end of the day, critical race theory is just that: a theory. And it should remain solely a theory in our schools. I am confident that anyone who examines it rationally will find CRT severely wanting." (Woodson, 2021)

I agree with all three of these distinguished scholars, but the problem is the leadership of the Teachers Unions and School Administrations that are now openly Marxist. They have forgotten what education is. Education is opening minds to critical thinking, not indoctrination. Putting the word Critical in front of a noun does not automatically make it anything worthwhile. It is the outcome that is important. The outcome of Education is supposed to be a student prepared for the transition to a useful life, to be useful to oneself, one's family and society at large. Not to be useful to the Collective and then be discarded. That is Marxist Socialism.

REFOCUS ON FACE-TO-FACE EDUCATION

If public schools exist truly to serve all students equally and inclusively, then we have to rebuild the seated class and increase the opportunity for extracurricular experiences. The use of online instruction that exploded after COVID was a failure. It diminished student engagement and pulled most teachers out of the classroom. The need for distancing was thought to be to protect the students and the teachers from the virus. But students were actually at low risk and with proper PPE, the teachers were safe. But contrary to logic the NEA and AFT resisted the return to in-person classroom instruction. Perhaps even more damaging than the closed classrooms was the effect at home. With suicide, opioid addiction, child abuse and neglect all being reported on the rise in a post-COVID world, all schools should return to full time instruction with limited in-class distractions as soon as possible. The Teachers Union's "we're here for you, but you cannot come to school or spend any time with your peers" has been destructive physically and mentally to students. It is clear that the Union leadership is selfishly anti-student. There can be no other explanation. The safest place during the Pandemic could have been the classroom.

"To serve all students equally and inclusively, the local schools must rapidly move far away from any program, practice or initiative that divides its students into categories based on their immutable characteristics. That is Critical Race Theory. Promoting the idea that some individuals achieve while others do not based on some inherent privilege or lack thereof is simply adhering to the bigotry of low expectations." (Eoff, 2021) If our public schools exist truly to serve all students equally and inclusively, they must incentivize good teachers to teach and good leaders to lead at the individual school level. Local schools should reinstitute disciplinary policies to ensure a positive, safe educational environment for the students and families who want to be in the public schools. Parents should be able to enroll their children in private (charter) schools without penalty and their tax contribution to education should be made available to them. The public schools should offer more in-house technical, vocational, trade and workforce training programs to help all students have a better chance finding meaningful work and purpose as they enter adulthood.

GET INVOLVED

Mark Levin says we must get proactive. "In every school district in America, local committees of patriotic community activists must organize, as some are already doing. Among other things, they should get involved in virtually every aspect of local public education. We can no longer leave the education of our children and the well-being of our community to "the professionals"." (Levin, 2021)

STAND UP FOR AMERICAN VALUES

It begins with you. You cannot stay on the couch and watch your Homeland reject its own Founding principles. My recommendation is for you to get involved in the process in any way that you can. Support conservative politicians and hold them accountable. Run for political office. Vote. Write. Speak-up at the local school board meetings and the PTA.

The following is from Chapter 6 of my first book, *The Moral Case for American Freedom:* "It is time to revisit the Founding Documents from a modern perspective. Now that may sound progressive. It's not really. We just want to look at these documents from our current perspective, not revise them. We need to glean the wisdom from what was written down, *when it was written down.* Let's begin by updating the first Document of Freedom, the Declaration of Independence. The following is not the original Declaration of Independence. It has been updated using a little of Thomas Paine's Common Sense and a look at today's political situation.

THE DECLARATION OF INDEPENDENCE (AGAIN)

There comes a time in the course of history of a free country when it becomes necessary for the governed to express their grievances with the government. It is the right of the people to expect the government to consider the grievances, make corrections to redress the grievances, or be replaced by another government. It is not the government's role to elevate its position above the people and force change on the people based on an elitist view. While it may be obvious to all, the self-evident truth may need repeating. It is the people who are "created equal, that they are endowed by their Creator with certain unalienable Rights, that among these are Life, Liberty and the pursuit of Happiness.

The People of the United States of America have agreed to be governed as a representative republic, not a democracy. The people of each state are supposed to be represented in a fair manner. It was originally only as a matter of convenience that the People of the United States of America consented to leave the legislative part of government to be managed by a select number chosen from each state by the people of each state through the process of state elections or state legislative appointments. Those selected were supposed to have the same concerns at stake as those who elected them with the expectation that those selected would act in the same manner as the whole body would act were they present. These elected or appointed representatives must never develop a self-interest separate from the state electorate.

Experience has pointed out the propriety of having elections often. Those previously elected can then return and mix again with the people. In a few months, their loyalty to the public would be reaffirmed since it would be clear to all that those previously elected had not made a cent for themselves. It was not the intent to establish a political profession.

And as this frequent interchange would establish a common interest with every part of the community, the elected and the governed would mutually and naturally support each other. On this depends the strength of the government and the happiness of the governed. As it is written under law, so let it be done. But it should always be understood that it is because of The Constitution of the People, not the Constitution of the Government, that the law is not oppressive.

Whenever any Form of Government becomes destructive of these ends, it is the Right of the People to alter or to abolish it, and to institute new Government, laying its foundation on such principles and organizing its powers in such form, as to them shall seem most likely to affect their Safety and Happiness.

Prudence and commonsense dictate that a long-established government should not be changed for light and transient causes. It can be shown that the People are more disposed to suffer, while evils are sufferable, than to right themselves by abolishing the forms to which they are accustomed. But when a long train of abuses and usurpations, pursuing invariably the same objective evinces a design to reduce them to a collective, then it is their right, it is their duty, to throw off such Government, and to provide new Guards for their future security.

Such has been the patient sufferance of nearly one half of the People, those in the Heartland of America who oppose absolute socialism and have been disenfranchised by a marginally corrupt government and conspiratorial, established liberal media. The history of the United States since the early 1900s is a history of incremental social engineering projects, all having the direct objective of establishing an absolute socialistic state. The Citizens of the United States of America renounce this socialistic objective.

WHAT CAN WE DO?

The preceding IS NOT the Declaration of Independence as written and signed on July 4, 1776. It is a new Declaration of Independence aimed at today's Government.

This new Declaration has three main objectives. It is pointing out the corruption that occurs with a "political profession". It is denouncing Progressivism. And it is justifying the replacement of an overreaching totalitarian Administrative State when necessary. The elected Government officials of the United States of America are not the real culprits, although they are complicit. The problem is the *unelected* Administrative State bureaucrats appointed by these elected officials. But it is the Biden Administration and the Democratic Party's pursuit of Progressivism that has now over-reached and that is what needs to be rejected and replaced. It is time to do just that. It begins with you and the Common Sense of the people of the American Heartland.

ABOUT THE AUTHOR

Martin Capages, Jr. is a retired professional engineer, technical executive and an Army veteran. His technical and management experience includes aircraft design, petroleum exploration and production, computer modeling and technology applications and structural engineering. He began writing political commentary in 2009 and completed his first book, *The Moral Case for American Freedom*, in July 2017. His writing is from the perspective of an engineer, Christian layman, conservative and Constitutional originalist.

Martin is married to Pamela Kay Capages. They have five children and seven grandchildren. Both Martin and Pamela are active members of their local Baptist church and serve in other state and international Christian ministries. Pamela is an author in her own right and has published books of poetry concerning her Christian faith, family and personal observations of nature.

REFERENCES AND WORKS CITED

Bannister, C. (2019, September 5). *Gov. Bevin on Gun Violence: 'What Has Changed? We, As a Culture...We Don't Value Human Life'*. Retrieved from www.cnsnews.com: https://www.cnsnews.com/blog/craig-bannister/gov-bevin-gun-violence-what-has-changed-we-culturewe-dont-value-human-life

Berenson, A. (2020). *UNREPORTED TRUTHS ABOUT COVID-19 AND LOCKDOWNS Part 3: Masks.* New York: Blue Deep Inc.

Capages Jr., M. (2017). *The Moral Case for American Freedom.* Springfield, Missouri: American Freedom Publications LLC.

Capages Jr., M. (2018). *HEARTLAND REBELLION.* Springfield, Missouri: American Freedom Publications LLC.

Capages Jr., M. (2020). *OF OSTRICHES AND LEMMINGS: The Silliness of Climate Change Hysteria.* Springfield, Missouri: American Freedom Publications LLC.

Capages Jr., M. (2020). *PERSISTENT EVIL: SOCIALISM.* Springfield, Missouri: American Freedom Publications LLC.

Capages Jr., M. (2021). *HEARTLAND RISING: The Defense of American Values.* Springfield, Missouri: American Freedom Publications LLC.

Cherry, R. R. (2018). *Restoring the American Mind.* Springfield, MIssouri: American Freedom Publications LLC.

Eoff, C. (2021, July 25). *SPS promotes inequity for equity's sake.* Retrieved from news-leader.com: https://www.news-leader.com/story/opinion/2021/07/25/sps-promotes-inequity-equitys-sake/8058900002/

Epstein, A. (2019, January 12). *Why Green Energy Means No Energy.* Retrieved from industrialprogress.com: http://industrialprogress.com/why-green-energy-means-no-energy/

Levin, M. R. (2021). *AMERICAN MARXISM.* New York: Simon and Schuster.

May, A. (2020). *POLITICS & CLIMATE CHANGE: A History.* Springfield, Missouri: American Freedom Publications LLC.

Mironuck, L. G. (2017). *Irreconcilable Differences.* Waynesville, Missouri: Lafayette Publishers.

Woodson, R. S. (2021, July 23). *A Better Way to Fight Critical Race Theory.* Retrieved from www.nationalreview.com: https://www.nationalreview.com/2021/07/a-better-way-to-fight-critical-race-theory/?mc_cid=14a06f2fc5&mc_eid=b0dd1c71dc

OTHER AMERICAN FREEDOM PUBLICATIONS LLC

AUTHOR OFFERINGS

By Martin Capages Jr. PhD

BOOTS TO BOGIES TO BRONZE: The Authorized World War II Biography of 2LT Jack C. Pyatt

THE MORAL CASE FOR AMERICAN FREEDOM

OZARK COUNTY HEART: Boyhood Memories of a Dora Missouri Farm

A WAKEFUL WATCH: The Authorized Biography of Charles Lindbergh Armstrong

HEARTLAND REBELLION

THE SILENT SECOND: The Biography of Martin Capages-Captain USMC

EPIPHANY: Before Time Zero- Faith of an Engineer

WHY THE GREEN NEW DEAL IS A BAD DEAL FOR AMERICA

FREEDOM OR SOCIALISM? The Millennial Dilemma

STARBOARD TACK: The Free Nation Makes a Course Correction

OF OSTRICHES AND LEMMINGS: The Silliness of Climate Change Hysteria

PERSISTENT EVIL—SOCIALISM: A Warning for the Millennial Generation

SHOW-ME WARRIOR O. K. Armstrong of Missouri

HEARTLAND RISING: The Defense of American Values

By Pamela Kay Capages

POEMS BY PAMELA

WILDWOOD PSALMS

By Ronald R. Cherry MD

RESTORING THE AMERICAN MIND

By Orland Kay Armstrong

OLD MASSA'S PEOPLE: The Old Slaves Tell Their Story

www.ingramcontent.com/pod-product-compliance
Ingram Content Group UK Ltd.
Pitfield, Milton Keynes, MK11 3LW, UK
UKHW022241230426
12048UKWH00018BA/1392